Love Is a Funny Thing

Love Us a

Funny Thing

By Dean Walley

Illustrated by
Stan Tusan

👑 Hallmark Editions

Love is a funny thing.
You'll see!
If you're going on seven
or seventy-three....

It's the thing in the movies
that looks kind of crazy...
the bright memory
when all others get hazy.
Love is a funny thing.

Love is a funny thing.
It's mush!
The guys are all great
and the girls
make you blush.
Life's an adventure
and love is a bore ...

till a 12-year-old vision
moves in right next door!
Love is a sweet
young thing.

Love is a funny thing.
It's great? You're
too old for your dolls
but too young for a date.
And love is a mystery,
   dark and unknown...
till the first time you hear
   his voice on the phone!
Love is a sunny thing!

Love is as sudden
as a summer shower...
as slow as
an unfolding flower...
back and forth—
a yo-yo on a string.

Love fools you
into feeling tragic...
next thing you know
it's making magic,
filling February up
with spring!

Love is a funny thing.
How true!
It's a magical
bibbity- bobbity- you.

You meet your
Prince Charming
on Yellow Brick Road...
then you give him a kiss
and find out he's a toad!
Love's an elusive thing.

Love is a funny thing.
Hooray!
It makes happy music
come strummin' your way.
It makes you feel tall
when you're only
                    five - eight...

then you're out on a date
and she tells you it's late!
Love is a fickle thing.

Love is a funny thing.
Unplanned.
    He's lost and alone.
She's not in demand.
But while frantically
searching for someone
    "who'll do"...

they run into each other
and out of the blue
they're in love...
that wonderful thing.

Love's downhill —

up

it's up —
up

                    warious...

grand illusion —

                truly glorious.

Your spirits sink —

then you begin to soar!

Hard to catch—
   so undependable,
but luckily
our hearts are mendable...
and all we really ask
   of love is <u>more</u>!

Love is a funny thing.
Disarming.
You're off
on your honeymoon —
everything's charming.
But going back home
to that one-room
apartment...

you start thinking
just how long
"till death do us part"
meant...

for love's an everyday thing.

Love is a funny thing.
Revealing.
And marriage exposes
each flaw
you're concealing.
It lets you hear snores;
lets you see every wart...

but still
    it can show you
  the depths of a heart.
Love is a growing thing.

Love is a funny thing.
    For two!
Then all of a sudden
        there's somebody new...
somebody hungry
and angry and screaming...

    someone you love
with a joy beyond dreaming.
Love is a tender thing.

The comedy, the melodrama
can cause a coma
or a trauma...
make you quit —
or go back to — a vice

Can't prevent it—
  there's no cure—
but catch it once
  and you'll be sure:
a bout of love that lingers
  can be _nice_!

Love is a funny thing.
It's numbing.
    You go out to dinner
and talk about plumbing.
And the years start
to fly—there's no time
    for romancing...

then a hand touches yours
and next minute
    you're dancing.
Love is a lovely thing.

Love is a funny thing.
It's silly.
Your lives are devoted
to Mike, Sue and Billy.
The disposer's not working
your savings get flatter.

but still...
    there are moments
when nothing else matters.
    Love is a "hold me" thing.

Love is a funny thing.
   A riot!
You're both past your prime
   and in need of a diet.
But — once in a while —
all alone — there's a look...

that puts down the knitting
   and closes the book.
Love is the only thing.

Love is a funny thing.
You know...
'cause love makes you hⁱg^h,
and it makes you feel l
o
w.

It's allofasudden!
Next minute it's not.
It's cold and it's hot,
but it's all
that we've got...

for love is a funny thing,
a shower and sunny thing,
bitter one minute,
then sweeter than honey...

...love is elusive — for sure —
   inconclusive,
      wonderful, tender,
a dream, a remember,
   knowing and glowing,
dreaming and growing...

      love is a funny —
the every- and-only thing.

Set in Two, a light, informal script
designed exclusively for Hallmark.
Typography by Hallmark Photo Composition.
Printed on Hallmark Eggshell Book paper.
Designed by William M. Gilmore and Beth Hedstrom.